Looking at Animal Parts

Let's Look at Animal Feet

by Wendy Perkins

Consulting Editor: Gail Saunders-Smith, PhD

Consultant: Suzanne B. McLaren, Collections Manager
Section of Mammals, Carnegie Museum of Natural History
Edward O'Neil Research Center, Pittsburgh, Pennsylvania

Capstone press

Mankato, Minnesota

Pebble Plus is published by Capstone Press,
151 Good Counsel Drive, P.O. Box 669, Mankato, Minnesota 56002.
www.capstonepress.com

1 2 3 4 5 6 11 10 09 08 07 06

Library of Congress Cataloging-in-Publication Data
Perkins, Wendy, 1957–
　　Let's look at animal feet / by Wendy Perkins.
　　p. cm.—(Pebble plus. Looking at animal parts)
　　Summary: "Simple text and photographs present animal feet, how they work, and how different animals
use them"—Provided by publisher.
　　Includes bibliographical references and index.
　　ISBN-13: 978-0-7368-6352-0 (hardcover)
　　ISBN-10: 0-7368-6352-4 (hardcover)
　　1. Foot—Juvenile literature.　I. Title. II. Series.
QL950.7.P47 2007
591.47'9—dc22   2006001002

Editorial Credits
Sarah L. Schuette, editor; Kia Adams, set designer; Renée Doyle, cover production; Kelly Garvin, photo
　　researcher/photo editor

Photo Credits
Corbis/W. Wayne Lockwood, M. D., 13
Getty Images Inc./The Image Bank/GK Hart/Vikki Hart, 6–7; Photonica/GK & Vikki Hart, cover
James P. Rowan, 8–9
Lynn M. Stone, 20–21
McDonald Wildlife Photography/Joe McDonald, 1, 10–11, 16–17
Minden Pictures/Frans Lanting, 14–15
Pete Carmichael, 19
Robert McCaw, 4–5

Note to Parents and Teachers

The Looking at Animal Parts set supports national science standards related to life
science. This book describes and illustrates animal feet. The images support early readers
in understanding the text. The repetition of words and phrases helps early readers learn
new words. This book also introduces early readers to subject-specific vocabulary words,
which are defined in the Glossary section. Early readers may need assistance to read
some words and to use the Table of Contents, Glossary, Read More, Internet Sites, and
Index sections of the book.

Table of Contents

Feet at Work

Animals use their feet
to get where
they want to go.

A duck paddles
across a pond.
Its two webbed feet
push the water
back and forth.

A heron walks

along the shore.

Its long toes

keep it from sinking

in the mud.

Kinds of Feet

Bears walk flat on their feet.

Pads of skin protect their feet

from sharp sticks and stones.

Donkeys have hoofed feet.

They walk on tiptoe.

Kangaroos can't walk
on their long feet.
They hop from place
to place instead.

Geckos have sticky feet.

They jump and cling to trees.

Parrots have clawed feet.
They wrap their feet
around tree branches.

Awesome Animal Feet

Large or small,

wide or narrow,

feet help animals move.

Glossary

clawed feet—animal feet with curved nails; claws can be sharp and pointy.

cling—to stick to or hold on to something very tightly

hoofed feet—animal feet with a hard outer covering; horses, deer, sheep, and other animals have hoofed feet.

protect—to keep safe

webbed feet—animal feet with skin that connects the toes together

Read More

Hall, Peg. *Whose Feet Are These? A Look At Hooves, Paws, and Claws.* Whose Is It? Minneapolis: Picture Window Books, 2003.

Miles, Elizabeth. *Legs and Feet.* Animal Parts. Chicago: Heinemann Library, 2003.

Swanson, Diane. *Animals Can Be So Speedy.* Animal Locomotion. New York: Greystone Books, 2001.

Internet Sites

FactHound offers a safe, fun way to find Internet sites related to this book. All of the sites on FactHound have been researched by our staff.

Here's how:

1. Visit *www.facthound.com*

2. Choose your grade level.

3. Type in this book ID **0736863524** for age-appropriate sites. You may also browse subjects by clicking on letters, or by clicking on pictures and words.

4. Click on the **Fetch It** button.

FactHound will fetch the best sites for you!

Index

Word Count: 113
Grade: 1
Early-Intervention Level: 14